While I'm Getting Naked

Here's My Shorts, Devotionals, and Poetry Filled Life Lessons & Bonus Journal Journey

By

Shemekka Ebony

Shemekka Ebony

Copyright © 2021 Shemekka Ebony

The scanning, uploading, copying, or distribution of this book without permission from the Author is prohibited. For permission to use this book (other than for review purposes), please contact shemekka@iambrilliant.org.

Thank you for honoring author's rights.

ISBN: 978-1-7371354-0-1

Published by ©2021 Kingpen Publishing House

Thank You

I want to thank you for your interest in this book. If you are reading this, it is purposed. It just may be that you find yourself on these pages, or find an answer for a friend. This is a compilation of my pain, curiosity and frustrations through my journey from being bitter to being better transformation. I have shared my journey with you in anecdotes, short stories, devotionals, and poems I have written through the years. It's a testament of what I have survived, and a memoir of my exodus from being bitter to having a better mindset. I pray it makes you smile, think, laugh, and reflect. There are so many angels I found along the way that have influenced this book. I am sure you will find yourself. May God bless you exceedingly as you grow comfortable getting naked about your lived experiences and learn to not feel ashamed. Take time to journal while you read, study the recommended scriptures, and find yourself becoming wiser along your life's journey.

Dedication

This book is dedicated to every person who has ever been told that you have a book inside of you. You may have a desire to write your story, but do not know where to begin. Start with this book. You never know how this reflective and inspiring journey can illuminate the spark that starts your book. It took me several years to release this book. Originally written in 2012 and now published in your hands. My excuses would tell me, *I'm not there mentally anymore*, and I thought it was a bleeding testimony that needed to be rewritten. That was the last illusion I had to destroy. Just because I wasn't in that space anymore, did not negate the power of the revelation of the journey. That's what nakedness and growth feel like. Journaling this life's journey helped me grow comfortable with my nakedness. I declare this literary release will help you too. -Shemekka Ebony

Bonus Journal Journey & Reflection- Note the prompts labeled Reflection and Journal. I encourage you to reflect and journal while reading.

Wellbeing Affirmation:

Speak this aloud:

Today is the First Day of my next life *in* God and *with* God. Today I make a decision to look beyond the past letting go of the hurts, anger, the frustrations, the fears, and failures.

Today I will put my trust not in myself or any other created being, but in the Creator alone; the Father of all who believe. Today I declare I am a believer!
(Author unknown)

And whenever I fall short of this declaration, I will return to it, check in with my feelings and declare it over my thoughts and life again!

Shemekka Ebony

Table of Contents

Part I: I'm Coming Out

Secret Place   9

Exodus: Healing Writings   11

I'd Like To Report A Robbery   14

Has Anyone Heard From Isaac   16

What's Your Resolution To End Empty Promises?   19

Name That Label   20

Part II: *Naked and Not Ashamed*

Hold'em or Fold'em   22

I Have Fallen and I Can't Get Up: The Illusion   23

Ways Of An Eagle: How Two Became One   25

Vegas Nuggets   26

The Rock, The Atheist, & The Mile   28

Part III: *Acts*

Ruling & Reigning	32
10 Things I Survived	33
Stop, Drop, & Roll	34
Don't Fall For It	36
Shake Your Snake	39
Therapeutic Release	41
Who Am I?	**43**

Part I
I'm Coming Out

Secret Place (Psalm 91)

He that dwelleth in the Secret Place of the Most High shall abide under the shadow of the almighty. – Psalm 91

Reflecting on this scripture, I first had to repent because I realized how much I would only *visit* God in the Secret Place mentioned above. I would take my baggage, challenges, and troubles and check into the Secret Place. I'd stay awhile, and when I feel refreshed, I would check out of the Secret Place; taking the same old baggage with me. I'd gain enough strength to feel a little more empowered to carry the load.

I got tired of that visitation routine and I asked God how I could unpack and take residence in this Secret Place described in Psalm 91? How do I begin to get comfortable? It is only when I learn to dwell, that I can really feel that empowerment that lasts longer than through my last storm. These temporary fixes aren't enough to sustain my walk. It's more to this relationship than just visiting God's safe space. God designed us with purpose! I, too often, would find myself checking in and checking out of Psalm 91 dwelling place. I had not been thinking that I could become a resident of His Secret Place.

Best thing about it, is I can leave all my baggage at the door, because He gives peace as clothing, the word as nourishment, and scents our atmosphere with the comforts of knowing that He supplies and provides for all of our needs according to His riches in Glory.

So it is in this moment, I invite you to join me in the Secret Place. This time knowing that I'm not checking out and you are welcome to also dwell within your Psalm 91.

Reflection: Read Psalm 91 and reflect in your journal.

Exodus: Healing Writings (Exodus 16)

A few years back I went through some things. I felt the weight of the world crumble the essence of my joy filled existence. I still don't know how I survived and how God restored me during that time, **but for His Grace**.

Emotionally I was shattered, physically I was drained and stressed. This pain was brought on by things I was experiencing in my marriage. My husband (at that time) was arrested for felony drug trafficking two months after birthing our second son. I couldn't figure out why God let that happen to me, us, our family. I wrestled with why my protector made decisions that put our family at risk. It was a hard journey carrying that internal fight within while he served nearly 6 year prison term. It was hard managing raising two sons without their father present. I felt condemned as a bad person and I had no role in what my ex-husband did. This judgment didn't come from all people around me you see, but stemmed from a group of friends and family that I considered significant at that time. I was holding on to pain connecting to believing they would be there for us and my limited capacity to express what I needed that to look like.

I was beginning to feel that maybe I was this "bad" person I was being painted to be. My friends tried to reach out for me but the person they were used to wasn't there. I became bitter and argumentative with the accusers trying to validate my feelings to a crowd of stone-throwers. When journaling about this, I felt self-condemnation and angry feelings were also rooted in my need for validation that I was being heard. I felt *if they knew my side maybe things would be different.* I thought, *if they knew my truth* maybe I could really heal, knowing that they heard me and my version of the experience. God brought the people out of Egypt in this scripture. They complained asking God why they couldn't have died in the comforts of Egypt instead of where Moses had brought them. It also made me think of Jesus on the path to the Cross. I imagined Jesus walking that path. Not once did Jesus stop and plea his innocence. Yet He knew the truth, while people cursed, stoned, and ridiculed Him, He walked forward in knowing the purpose and the Victory.

Now, I'm not comparing myself to being as faultless as Jesus here, just noting there may be times that there are crosses we have to carry for purposes greater than us and there is no time to stop and be heard along the way. Sit with that a moment. In this moment, I conceive my healing and invite you to yours also. No longer will our healings be harnessed by the need to be heard or validated.

During my painful journey, I chose to become better and not bitter about what God chose in my exodus journey. Though bitterness was justified, there was no space for it in my new dwelling place. I took my Exodus from this harness of validation-seeking. I'm a better woman today than I ever was before. I didn't make perfect decisions, I made survivor moves. Thanks be to God, I no longer have to live in survivor mode. I can unpack in the Secret Place. During my Exodus, I had to declare my freedom. I Declare I am free, I am promise. As I learn my new identity of freedom, I am leaving behind bondage. I will not be tempted back into a mentality of bondage. I will resist.

Reflecting on my Exodus, I'm grateful for those that have witnessed my *wandering;* provided my *manna* provisions, heard my complaints, and covered me thru it all. We all need someone to witness, provide, and cover us while in development through our exodus experiences.

Journal Reflection: What is your Exodus? What character would you have been in the wilderness? Imagine a conversation with Moses.

Shemekka Ebony

I'd like to report a robbery! (Philippians 4:8)

During one of my mentoring sessions I realized something about myself. I could recognize that there was at least one person in my life that I didn't seem to ever stay mad at, or remember why I should be upset. My response to justify my care for that one person was effortless to repeat I don't get mad at him because it takes too much energy to do so. I realized that though I have this seemingly with one person, I now have the opportunity to make this a standard and apply to all relationships in my life.

I began to think about how there are individuals that have upset me or still have the potential to. All it took was a triggered memory and the emotions & thoughts from that initial offense would rise. My face would begin to frown, gritting teeth, and body tensing at the thought of those individuals. And then the bad thoughts begin, how I was wronged, how I was scared, etc. Then the sulking stage, you know, the 'why me's and thoughts of revenge arise.

Whew, when I begin to realize how much of my energy is put into being angry at someone. I think of how I was robbing myself of this potential positive energy. My mentor helped me to reflect on how I was robbing God of positive energy and using that energy negatively. I gasped, he had a point! I immediately became Godly sorry unto repentance. God gives us reminders on how not to fall into traps of feeding energy to anger. Through the Word of God, we are encouraged to think on things that are pure, to cast your cares upon Him, and remembering in all things give thanks...etc. Yet I robbed that power to glorify God and gave myself away to evil thoughts and anger. We all may find ourselves feeling this negative energy at times. We have examples of pure love in God's word that can help us use energy for good to all and pursue peace among men.

When the presentation to be angry is set before us, we have a choice to pursue peace or stir up wrath. Making the decision to be better and not bitter is a conscious decision we should chose. In choosing to be better, we get to become a sweet offering before God. So next time you find yourself raising energy in anger, think about returning that energy to God and renewing your mind.

Reflection: What's robbing your mental space of thinking on things that are pure?

Shemekka Ebony

<u>Has Anyone Heard from Isaac? (Genesis 22)</u>

One early December some time ago, I listened in awe to one of my dear friends as he presented his father's eulogy. The sermon was *Has Anyone Heard From Isaac?* He shared revelation upon revelation all of which, I'm sure I won't be able to capture here, but I wanted to share a few that spoke volumes to me. He shared how Isaac helped his father Abraham prepare an offering unto God as found in Genesis 22. Isaac asked what the offering was, and Abraham replied, God will provide. I sat imagining with my friend as he shed light on the fact that Isaac was God's promise to Abraham in his old age. Also, Isaac was a mere teenager and Abraham was over 100 years old.

First revelation was about how Isaac had to choose to be the sacrifice while waiting on the offering. He spoke of the willingness of his countenance to obey his father, even as he lay still to be bound by him. I saw the miracle in the message in understanding that Abraham, whom was promised a son, was told to sacrifice him as an offering unto God. The very things God promised us, he may require us to offer it back to Him. Can you wait on a promise to manifest, see the promise, receive the promise, rejoice in the presence of the promise, and while you are rejoicing, be obedient to God's call in offering it back to God? Actually, the whole time, it wasn't just the promise God wanted back, it was the obedience in Abraham's spirit. His obedience caused an angel to appear and a ram in the bush to manifest. It was the YES of Isaac's spirit, his willingness to totally trust his father even when he didn't understand what was next.

While Getting Naked

See, Isaac was the chosen one, the promised seed of God. Yet feelings of him being the promised son went out the window for Abraham. He chose not to idolize his promise, in reminding God, it was His promise unto him. There are times in our lives when we know what God has willed for our lives, we know the promises he has declared for us. Yet, God wants us to love, believe, trust, and obey without hesitation. We make preparations in offering our money, or talents unto God and yet, He is seeking US to be the sacrifice, like Isaac, while waiting on the offering.

I walked away from that Home Going Celebration, desiring to not only release my gifts and talents, but also totally give myself. To offer back to God, that which He promised me. See because, I knew what God said, I held to those promises, I harnessed them; I boxed promises up and waited for the manifestation. All the while I was allowing my promises to become a distraction to my serving God. I knew there was better yet to come in my latter, yet I was doing nothing to get there. I guess I was banking on my promises more than the power of God to manifest it. I quickly repented for my actions and placed my promises along with my YES on the altar as an offering unto God. I refused to allow my promises to become my idol. I refused to allow my promises to become my distraction. I refused to allow my need for my promises to overpower my willingness to obey through my YES. I heard from Isaac that day-I decided to model Isaac's willing countenance to lie down, before God, as the offering until God sends the sacrifice.

Shemekka Ebony

Journal Ideas: Could you offer yourself willingly after noticing you may be the only one? Are you waiting on a promise to manifest? How has the delay affected your faith journey?

What's Your Resolution to End Empty Promises? (Matthew 5:37)

Have you set goals that tend to be dropped or forgotten by the end of the month? Do you set expectations which are hard to meet? Have you written your vision? Did you make a pathway to reach the goals?

Start by making a short term goal for today.

1. Think of something you would like to do today.
2. Write out a schedule of what you know you have to do, then fill in where you can fit in that goal.
3. Once you accomplish that goal-
    a. Celebrate it
    b. Study how you did it.
4. Now ease out and set a goal for this weekend, write a vision (schedule) to accomplish it and celebrate the victory.

Moral: Goals without a vision/schedule is just a potential dream.

Journal Idea: Follow the plan above and commit.

Shemekka Ebony

Name that Label (James 4:11-12)

Many of us wear labels that we either were born with, earned, or were given by life's traumatic experiences or crisis. Make a list of all the labels you wear or are overcoming. You may have labels like sister, mom, dad, liar, cheater, promiscuous, hetero/homosexual, strong, meek etc.

Journal: Now that you have made a list of labels you wear.

1. Choose your top three and reflect on why these are important to you. If you have more than three that you identify with, go further.
2. If there are labels you came up with that are misrepresentations of whom you are or not who you want to be known as, I'd recommend you take those labels and reassign it back to the person who gave it to you.

Use this exercise to release yourself from the labels that feel like harnesses too. As you let go, write a goodbye letter/note/declaration to that label. Turn and don't look back. If you feel inclined to grab that label again, revisit your goodbye note and really believe old things are passed away.

Part II
Naked & Not Ashamed

Shemekka Ebony

Hold'em or Fold'em (Proverbs 3:5)

Texas Hold'em was my cell phone game of choice. It is a game of chance and wit where you decide between bidding, going blind, fold or bluff. You start with two cards and make bets on whether you can make suits out of the cards not yet seen. If you do not get dealt strong cards in the beginning, you face having to "fold" to avoid risk of loss. It's a calculated decision based on how "strong" the cards are, how good your opponents are, and how much of your money you will risk.

In reflection, I'd like to liken this game to relationships and decisions we have to live with. Are the relationships you are in right now, established on a calculated risk assessment? The decisions you make, are they "bluff", "blind", or "all in" ordeals? Did you seek God about it? What does God have to say about you going in giving Him bluff promises? Did you make God some "blind" commitments that you did not follow through with? Are you really "all in" or is this just for this hand (relationship, situation, convenience)?

Journal: Write about your "bluff", "blind", and "all in" status. How will you play the hand you are dealt as a result of what you bring to the table?

I've Fallen and I Can't Get Up. (Romans 3:23)
Ten Imaginations (2 Corinthians 10:5)

As I had another experience in the workshop I call *the church* this morning this is what was revealed to me! (Please note that sometimes you can be somewhere like church and two different messages are taught. One message is from the teacher, and one you also receive from God while you are there. I begin putting this together yesterday, but this service experience brought it out for me today.

Too often falling becomes some type of cliché' we use when we err from our path of righteousness. It's not always clear how others interpret your fall, so let me define: for those that may be reading this and don't really know me. I'm referring to falling by my definition: I often make choices contrary to God's plan for my life, which is when I believe I have fallen. I recently fell, but while I was down this time, I chose not to "get up" the same way. I began to really think about what it means to get up after falling. I frequently find that I'm ministering to people that feel condemned for "falling" long after they have asked for forgiveness from God. Here is your free *therapy session* feel free to put it in your own tool box!

The devil (in whatever form you identify him, *the enemy*, your ego (self), Satan...etc) sends us all kinds of illusions to keep us bound after we fall. These thoughts are then planted and grow, and we base our future actions on it, as well as our view of our relationship with God and others. So here are my Ten Illusions the devil may present to hinder your *getting up* from falling. I would give you scripture references, but you should really seek scriptures that connect to your own Imaginations, have you been believing a lie? Let's save that for the journaling. "Thy word have I hidden in my heart, that I might not sin against you (Psalm 119:11)."

Ten Imaginations You May Have Believed
(fill in the blanks to reflect your truths)
1. You don't want to do this_____ (Faith, trust, God) thing anymore, just quit.
2. You can't overcome this _____.
3. How can you ask for forgiveness? You wanted this to happen.
4. No need to repent, you are going to do it again.
5. Don't go to church, you know you can't feel God with _____ on your mind.
6. How can you worship, knowing what you did?
7. You are unfit to serve, pray for, minister in church, home, community, or office.
8. There is no good thing in you, you can't do right.
9. You might as well stop praying, God doesn't hear a sinner's prayer.
10. Just give up trying. This saved life isn't for you. It was easier back when you _____.

Journal Idea: So *snap* if you can relate and personalize this with the illusions masking as crippling truths. Then find your truth in scripture and debunk those illusions. All the answers can be found between Genesis and Revelation.

The Ways of an Eagle: Two Became One (Genesis 2:24)

There is a story that describes a way of an eagle I remember hearing from early college. A game of tag between the male and female Eagle begins. This could last for days. The female Eagle takes a stick up in the air, approximately 8 to 10 thousand feet in a three dimensional figure eight pattern, and she then requires the male Eagle to catch the stick before it touches the ground. The male Eagle has to then return the stick back to the female Eagle. Then the female Eagle, each time, flies a little lower and faster with a larger stick. The game climaxes when the female Eagle is less than five hundred feet from the ground and she releases the stick. At this point, the male Eagle has to catch the stick before it touches the ground or the female Eagle will chase the male Eagle off. If the male Eagle catches the stick, he satisfies the female Eagle in knowing that when they have baby Eaglets he will be able to catch the Eaglets when teaching them how to fly thus assuring her that he will make a fit partner.

Journal Idea: For the singles: Can you carry yourself? Can you carry a family? Do you get tired and quit easily? Do you give up? Are you up for the challenges as you seek for God to show you whom you are spending forever with.

For the married: Are you continuing to pursue your mate as strongly as you did in the beginning? Are you dating your mate while married?

Shemekka Ebony

<u>Vegas Wisdom (Proverbs 4:7)</u>

I had just returned from Vegas, which I will never call Sin City again. It's something how one small Vegas Strip becomes such a large city's negative identifier. Much like our life, we may be the one that got pregnant out of wedlock, the one that drank too much in college, the one labeled as easy, the one that acted too ___ (fill in the blank). We are so much more than what we have been through, or what errors we feel we have made in life; but enough of that. On my way to Vegas, I finally had some alone time with God on the plane. I also took the time to edify and exhort some of my friends traveling with me, in notes I wrote to them. It was my prayer that while writing those notes for them, that God illuminate something specific for them. Nevertheless, I had to take some of what was for them for my own development.

Now, I have no fear in flying. I have done it too often in my life. Yet the turbulence of this flight I guess triggered something which I heard so clearly for me. If I died today, my purpose would be unfulfilled. It is this reason I am confident and have no fear in death because even death has no power in my purpose. Even death has to submit to God's purpose manifested through me on Earth.

Now these are some nuggets that I gleaned from God for my traveling exhortation love notes to friends:

    1. Reflecting on what you have can always silence the voice of the "have-not" thoughts in your life. Be grateful in all you have.done, acquired, and fulfilled. When

life shows you your 'have-nots'. For example thoughts about what you 'have-not' finished, acquired, achieved.

 2. God sees us as HE intended us to be. It's us that spend our lives trying to figure out who that is. We should always be searching to discover who we are purposed to be. This keeps us striving for excellence, humble, and grateful.

 3. You are created in the Image of God. You are perfected through trials to sharpen your Image so that others can see what God looks like in you!

It's the God in me that makes me amazing and you are amazing too.

Journal Idea: What is your reflection with this scripture or devotion?

Shemekka Ebony

The Rock, The Atheist, & The Mile

This devotional journey happened all in one morning all the way to the gym:

The Rock

As I was driving to the gym a rock hit my windshield. Now this left a chipped mark which I was excited about cause I already have a huge crack from another rock that I "missed the insurance bus" on last year. A new insurance, new claim and same windshield. I was so happy. (I know, there are so many other ways to look at that) The gods pooped; someone shot at me, constipated bird, etc. I'm going to stick to the rock idea. Weeks ago I was saying out loud. Another rock needs to hit my windshield so I can get it replaced. Today the universe responded.

Message: Be careful how you use your words, God and the Universe are listening.

The Atheist

While watching a video on my cell phone while using the treadmill at the gym when the lady running beside me brought my attention to our then, newly appointed, 1st Lady Michelle Obama on TV. She asked, "Have you ever pondered that in 8 years, it has to be 8 years since President Obama will do two terms (unless he really screws up), that Michelle could run for president?" A light went on in my face, wow that would be cool. She said, "Really, she will have 8 years of hands on education and experience." I asked, *don't you have to be a senator or governor or something*, she said no. "Just have enough sense and confidence from the people to be able to understand and communicate with other countries as well as us." I thought. That would be so cool. She went on to share that if that occurred, that would take care of two of the three things she wants to see happen before she dies.

1. See a Black Man in the White house.

2. See a Woman in the White House.

3. See a Woman complete a mile in 4 minutes.

I looked at her meter (she has run over two miles, and got enough breath to talk to me!) and I said 'that could be you; you know'. I'm just working up to one mile, I thought, while speeding up. She said, "At 40 when I completed my first mile it was such a spiritual high to feel that mile behind you." She said, "See I'm atheist. I know every day is special, and I can't afford to waste any of it. My body was designed to be healthy and I am glorifying it when I keep it in its best health."

I was thinking, wow; we take our bodies for granted too often and neglect our health. I mean- believers believe that our bodies are our temple and the temple of the Holy Spirit, but we could care less about our body's condition as we binge on whatever our FLESH says.

Message in The Mile

During my mile, this lady taught me so much more than I could have gotten if I had not been in that place at that time.

5 Lessons Learned

1. Our bodies were designed to be healthy.
2. We glorify God when we are good stewards over our body.
3. Push yourself further than you think you can go, stretch your body, it kills your flesh.
4. Change your routine, we are creatures of habit. Break free, just say no (to that midnight snack)
5. A mile isn't that hard to do when you are not thinking about how hard a mile is to finish.

I finished that mile in no time, and kept going. I even got off the treadmill and walked the track as I gave God glory for the things he just released in my life through that woman. These 5 Lessons are appreciated and I pray for her. (note- to the Jesus enthusiasts who may read this and got lost at the statement on atheism, it was definitely not the place to convert her from her atheist status). I would have missed so much of what she gave me, if I would have primed up after her "I'm an atheist" statement. Actually, I don't believe she is atheist at all.

Journal Idea: What's your reflection?

Part III
Acts

Shemekka Ebony

Ruling and Reigning (Philippians 4:13)

I Can Do All Things

Don't waste time on making new resolutions. Let's make a New Covenant and Be the Resolution for God's people, the Nations, ministries, and the lost. Let's get a full understanding while making sure that we not enter another year of preparation. Let us walk into a year of Activation! There has been a season of prepared people awaiting travel into a prepared land.

This is not to say that God is not going to continue to develop us. In addition to our development, let our potentials now be transformed into kinetics. Potential is described as what someone could be doing if they applied themselves. The kinetic energy of an object is the extra energy which it possesses due to its motion. Kinetics is the energy that births/manifests movement. Declare for yourself that we are out of preparation season, and may our Kinetic energy be manifest in our renewed covenant of Ruling and Reigning in Righteousness!
Journal Idea:

Why not write out your vision-create your vision board! Place reminders around your house. Become the change you want to see! If you don't know who you are and what your giftings are by now, ask a mentor, a close friend, your pastor. No more wandering in the fields of uncertainty and indecision!

10 things I Survived

Ok here goes. When you feel like you are going through and can't make it. Make your own "I Survived" list for reflection. Each of these times, I thought I couldn't make it, but God! I'm here and stronger for it. We can make it to the other side of through together!

1. I survived Kinston and Simon Bright projects.
2. I survived mayonnaise sandwiches.
3. I survived toy-less Christmases.
4. I survived molestations and rapes.
5. I survived living without a father.
6. I survived being spanked.
7. I survived being promiscuous.
8. I survived feeling denied by people I trusted to lead me.
9. I survived being torn away from my mate.
10. I survived longing to take my own life.

This list is in no particular order of hierarchy, it's actually condensed. I take no credit for my survival. God and my purpose still have me here. And as I continue to seek both God and purpose, it will remain unfinished!

Journal Idea: What's your survival list?

Shemekka Ebony

Stop Drop & Roll (Hebrews 12:1-2)

Lay Aside Every Weight

So as I lay awake this morning tearful thinking of my family, dear friends, and time spent through the years, as well as what lies ahead. There is no doubt that I have seen my fair share of joy, pain, and tragedy. What came to mind is this: ever so often I find myself in a place which I conduct introspective assessments. My new assessment is this: It's time to Stop, Drop, and Roll.

Yeah, I had that same look too when it came to my mind, but hear me out. For me, there are things I need to *stop*, people I need to *drop*, and some situations I need to *roll* out of. For each of us, this journey will be different.

Life is not promised. Do not put off to tomorrow what you can accomplish today.

Journal Idea: Take a piece of paper:

1. Make three columns and title each column as follows. *Stop. Drop. Roll.*

2. List **people, ideas, fears, and other things** that have been weighing you down, holding you back, and causing you pain under each column.

*Please note, once you categorize it on paper; you must follow through with the action column you placed it under.

Level two can be sharing this with an accountability partner and working on this in prayer together!

Shemekka Ebony

Don't Fall For it (Matt. 4:9)

Now, I'm sure many of us believe our Pastor is the greatest in the world. I too believe that I have been blessed with a leader that has an ear to hear and puts his hands to the plow. He was ministering a series called Love Handles which was instrumental in a life change for me. Today he hit a side note during the sermon. A side note is a Speaker's way of noting a future sermon topic while giving the background for the current topic? Well today's future topic was birthed in Matt.4:9 *Don't Fall For It.* This was just leaping in my spirit so much that I had to birth what it was saying to me.

Matthew 4 speaks of Jesus' temptation after his fast. What has occurred before verse 9 is that Satan has made offerings to Jesus to tempt him from what God already promised. Satan reveals to Jesus a vision of many kingdoms and made an offer to Jesus that he can have them if he fell down and worshipped him. See, first off, Satan was out writing checks that he can't cash! In other words Jesus was being tempted with something he knew he should have or had been promised. All of which, he could have taken prematurely, and lost focus. Truth is that Jesus has dominion over those kingdoms already-it just wasn't his appointed time. He needed to carry the cross and become the Resurrection before the manifestation of the promise. Satan, can show us our future with a "bye"-passing of the trouble (the cross) which is what gets us the anointing to handle our future. Taking the "bye" pass in life gets us to our promised place prematurely with no power to sustain the promise. In other words, getting some glory, without having a story. Not so! Too long we have wanted our promised land/place and invited our "mess" to dwell there with us. And when the fire came to purify us for our promised place-we gave up and walked away. Now that's another sermon. Are we willing to be purified thru fire on our way to our promised place?

Let us get back to the topic. *Don't fall for it*. I'll talk about me, as this immediately sent me to a place of self reflection. I am converting into living a fasted and consecrated lifestyle. During my fast sessions, I found myself being tempted. It wasn't until today that I was able to view temptation differently. We often view temptation as something bad and sent to knock us down at our weak place-so we would fall in self defeating prophesy. It was never God's intention-nor was it His hand that tempted us. My mentor mentions that we are tempted where we are now to show us our deliverance or where we still need to be delivered. Even in our temptation we must resist the devil that he may flee. I can resist temptation from an empowered place and I can choose to overcome now and not fall because I feel weak.

Verse 9-Satan shows Jesus something that he doesn't have ownership to give. He is making shallow promises which he can't fulfill. Sound familiar? I'll talk about me in case it hasn't happened to you. Too often guys wrote me checks trying to get close, which they could not cash-even those that seem to cash checks, couldn't last. So too many times I was giving myself away to an empty promise, 20 minutes of fame, and moments of my life I couldn't take back. And I'd find myself falling for same lies, new faces; sending me back to the altar calling myself back together. Jesus has shown me here-that even when tempted with the things I desire, or with what is already promised to me-I can choose to say NO, until my appointed time. Just as Jesus, I know there are some promises that are mine, and I have seen them. Not until my appointed time, will I claim all that is mine.

Today I share with you this. You will be given many temptations. It is the purpose of sin to deter you from your promise. Next time you are given an offer that you know is not of God, don't fall for it! Is it worth you wandering the path of unrighteousness? Is it worth your anointing? Don't fall for it! Is it glorifying God? Don't fall for it! Is it a temporary fix? Don't fall for it! There are two letters which we all know too well, that answers the above stated questions. For me, the answer is No. This allows me to give my "yes" away to GOD and God alone. How about you?

Journal Ideas: Does this temptation glorify God? Is it a temporary fix? How can you stand as an over comer in these areas of temptation?

Shake your Snake!! (Acts 28 3:6)

This scripture describes when Paul was on the Island of Malta. He went to gather sticks and a venomous snake attached to Paul's hand. Immediately the people begin to guess his sin (as he was a prisoner on his way to Rome) as they awaited him to swell up and die. They conspired in judgment that this affliction was justice doing its work for his crime, which he could not escape. Paul shook off the snake into the fire and was unharmed. After a long wait for death, the people changed their minds and decided he was a god.

We all have snakes that attach themselves to us openly. Let me rewind. Snakes crawl on the ground. So ideally, the snake could have been just as successful attacking an ankle. But the people would not have easily seen him hanging! The intent of this exposed attack was to openly show people that Paul was in some way evil and for future reference, don't accept what Paul says, (silly devil). The snakes that openly attack us may be tragedy, disease, sickness, loss of job, unplanned pregnancy, divorce, or cancer. People seem to immediately say, I wonder what they did to cause this to happen. What sin is he/she 'paying for'? And God forbid if they know of you falling in the past, their mind immediately hastens to that to justify your current condition. Paul didn't have to defend himself; he didn't have to tell them that he was being wrongly persecuted, etc. He shook the snake (put it in its place-fuel for the fire), and let God be glorified in them seeing he was not harmed. See your snakes aren't all about you. It's to help others around you (prayerfully) grow in humility and recede in judgment.

First public example that comes to mind is what was said about God judging Haiti. The good news is that God is glorified even the more by the multitude of humanitarians all over the world that stepped up and came together in unity to assist those in need. Haiti's snake may have bitten hard, but the Power of God covers them and restores a nation by providing resources they have needed all along. So no need to defend your snake attack, SHAKE YOUR SNAKE OFF and be about your Father's business.

Journal Ideas:
Identify your snakes. What's your plan to shake?

Therapeutic Release

What I have learned:
A person sometimes chooses to stay defeated because of fear.
In a day, a loved one can be gone. Don't let life, your job, etc. distract you from what's most important.
One CAN cross color lines and embrace one another in love.
Love is who I am AND what I do.
One minute you can be on top of the world and the next you feel that you are the only one straining to hold it up. In a few hours- one's reality can drastically shift for the worst.

"Family" isn't those who are SUPPOSED to be there-- They are the ones who CHOSE to be there. And those don't always end up being blood relatives.
I can't think about what I don't have when I am holding on to all I have left.
You can't expect something out of someone who doesn't believe or know they are supposed to be/do something.
You will just hurt more. Either speak about what you need, or leave it alone.
Just a call to say hi or I'm thinking of you is better than saying 'I didn't call because I didn't know what to say'.
Your coworkers CAN be your best friends ever!
I'd rather sleep on the floor in a home with people that love me, than peep a nap in the presence of people I don't trust.

Prayer changes more than things.

Shemekka Ebony

"Love and Marriage" isn't a magic feeling or fairytale combination. It's a work in progress, if you are willing to do the work, you will reap manifesting the progress.

Journal Idea:

How did you feel reading these? Which stood out? What are some anecdotes you have learned?

Who Am I?

I am powerful beyond measure.

I am a compact/multipurpose/experiential treasure.

Life is my gift, relationships are a bonus.

I am loosed from the harness of pain & sorrow.

As I journey discovering my new existence, I absorb the treasure with a "Yes" as I maximize the experience.

I share myself as a gift to all whom seek to discover: The ever fulfilling testimony of me! A child, a leader, a wife, a mother. I am a living epistle-read by men daily!

Transformed within, able to live again-Glory to the one that made me! **– Shemekka Ebony**

Shemekka Ebony

Notes:

While Getting Naked

Notes:

Shemekka Ebony

Notes:

About the Author

Shemekka Ebony Stewart-Isaacs, Founder of Black Girl Magic Market, Co-Founder of I Am Brilliant, People with Lived Experience Institute, and the CROWN Campaign, Raleigh, NC

Shemekka Ebony is a Brilliant wife and mother of 6. Shemekka is a Community Engagement Strategy Expert, Health and Racial Equity leader, and a Johns Hopkins' Health Policy Research Scholar Leadership Coach, an initiative funded by Robert Woods Johnson Foundation.

Her faith is the forerunner for her life's works. She has been serving in *The Hedges & Highways*, Communities, and ministry for over 20 years. I Am Brilliant is her flagship for organizing and engagement strategies dedicated to connecting all the threads that weave through communities in order to provide people better access, honor their experiences, and institute better practices for sustainable partnerships. She works with her husband, Michael Stewart-Isaacs, co-founder of I Am Brilliant to consult several Community and National organizations for better practices in meaningful and authentic community engagement and leadership development. Connect at www.shemekkaebony.com

Shemekka Ebony

www.ingramcontent.com/pod-product-compliance
Lightning Source LLC
Chambersburg PA
CBHW071324080526
44587CB00018B/3340